Nature's Mysteries

MALDIVES' SEA OF STARS

by Patricia Hutchison

abdobooks.com

Published by Pop!, a division of ABDO, PO Box 398166, Minneapolis, Minnesota 55439.

Printed in the United States of America, North Mankato, Minnesota.

102020
012021

THIS BOOK CONTAINS RECYCLED MATERIALS

Cover Photo: Shutterstock Images
Interior Photos: Shutterstock Images, 1, 5, 7 (left), 7 (right), 8, 16, 17, 18, 19, 21, 23, 24, 28–29; iStockphoto, 6, 12–13, 25; E. R. Degginger/Science Source, 11; NASA, 15; Doug Perrine/ Nature Picture Library/Alamy, 26

Editor: Alyssa Krekelberg
Series Designers: Candice Keimig, Victoria Bates, and Laura Graphenteen

Library of Congress Control Number: 2020940279

Publisher's Cataloging-in-Publication Data

Names: Hutchison, Patricia, author.

Title: Maldives' sea of stars / by Patricia Hutchison

Description: Minneapolis, Minnesota : POP!, 2021 | Series: Nature's mysteries | Includes online resources and index

Identifiers: ISBN 9781532169182 (lib. bdg.) | ISBN 9781532169540 (ebook)

Subjects: LCSH: Islands--Maldives--Juvenile literature. | Lakes--Juvenile literature. | Phytoplankton--Juvenile literature. | Bioluminescence--Juvenile literature. | Curiosities and wonders--Juvenile literature. | Geography--Juvenile literature.

Classification: DDC 910.02--dc23

WELCOME TO DiscoverRoo!

Pop open this book and you'll find QR codes loaded with information, so you can learn even more!

Scan this code* and others like it while you read, or visit the website below to make this book pop!

popbooksonline.com/sea-of-stars

*Scanning QR codes requires a web-enabled smart device with a QR code reader app and a camera.

TABLE OF CONTENTS

CHAPTER 1

SWIMMING WITH THE STARS

Stars shine in the sky above the ocean. A swimmer waves his hand through the water. Tiny specks of light flash around him. A girl walks along the beach. She leaves sparkling footprints in the sand. Glowing blue waves lap behind her.

WATCH A VIDEO HERE!

Many visitors are amazed by the glowing water and sand seen in areas of the Maldives.

The Maldives is a group of tropical islands.

The beach is on Vaadhoo Island. This island is part of the Maldives. The Maldives is a country in the Indian Ocean. It's made up of more than 1,000 islands. Water near several islands can shimmer and glow. But the water around Vaadhoo Island is the most famous.

MAP OF THE MALDIVES

The tiny spots of light in the water look like stars.

Many people visit Vaadhoo Island every year. They come to see the glowing water. It's called the Sea of Stars. On dark nights, the sea seems to reflect an image of the sky above. Both are full of tiny, glowing lights.

FUN FACT

The sand near the Sea of Stars glows too. It looks like the stars are sitting on the beach.

CHAPTER 2

LIGHTING UP THE OCEAN

The sparkle in the Maldives' Sea of Stars comes from tiny **organisms** called **dinoflagellates** (dine-oh-FLAJ-uh-leyts). These creatures are also called fire plants. They have this name because

LEARN MORE HERE!

they light up. Fire plants are a type of **phytoplankton** (feye-toh-PLANGK-tuhn). Many fire plants live in water around the islands.

Fire plants are extremely small. Many can only be seen with a microscope.

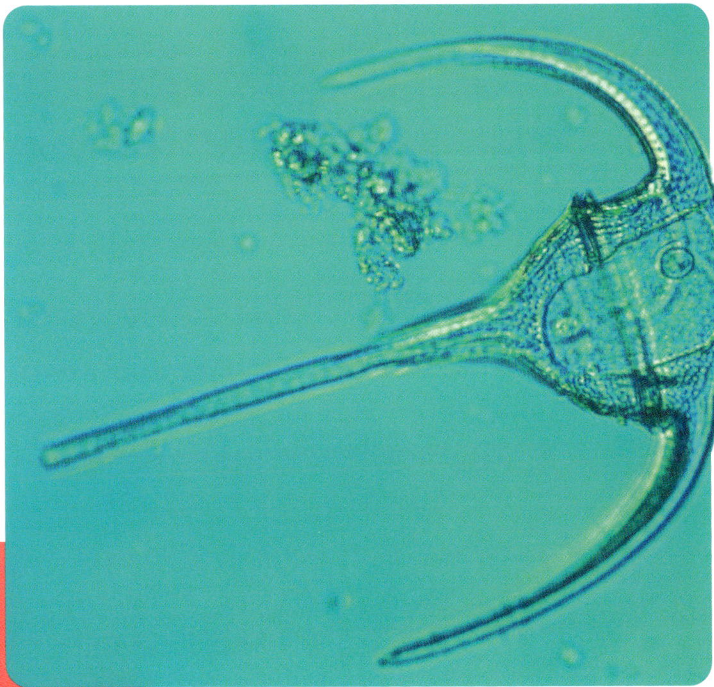

Fire plants are **bioluminescent** (bye-oh-loo-min-ESS-ent). That means they can create their own light. The light is produced when something disturbs the fire plants. This can be a wave or a fish.

If people step on fire plants in the sand, they will leave behind glowing footprints.

People can also make fire plants glow. If they move the water around with their hands or feet, the small creatures will light up.

GLOWING BRIGHTLY

Fire plants can cause large areas of the ocean to give off a blue glow. These areas are called milky seas. In 1995, a ship in the northwestern Indian Ocean passed through an area like this. Later, scientists found out that this milky sea was about the size of Connecticut. It glowed so brightly that it could be seen from space.

Millions of fire plants can live in one small section of water. The fire plants' glow is most noticeable on moonless nights. The darkness makes the lights in the sea look brighter.

Phytoplankton bloomed near France in the spring of 2013. Satellites in space took pictures of the colorful water.

FUN FACT

Fire plants also cause waters in Puerto Rico, California, Florida, and elsewhere to glow.

CHAPTER 3

FLICKERING FIRE PLANTS

Light travels in waves. When light waves reach the eye, the brain registers them as colors. Blue has a short wavelength.

Every color has a different wavelength.

Short wavelengths travel more easily through the water. That's why the Sea of Stars looks blue.

Light can travel underwater. Most light only reaches about 656 feet (200 m) deep.

COMPLETE AN ACTIVITY HERE!

The fire plants' flicker lasts only a fraction of a second. It is dependent on luciferin (loo-SIF-er-in). Luciferin is a chemical found inside a fire plant.

Glowworms in caves also have luciferin and glow blue.

A group of fire plants makes large sections of water glow blue.

The fire plants can flash many times before all the luciferin has been used. They recharge the next day through **photosynthesis**. Then, they light up again at night.

Scientists believe fire plants flash to defend themselves. The light is like a burglar alarm. When a **predator** is near, the fire plant lights up. The glow scares off the predator. It saves the fire plant from being eaten.

FUN FACT

If a small creature, such as a shrimp, eats a fire plant, its stomach will glow. The shrimp then becomes a target for bigger predators.

Some small fish eat fire plants.

CHAPTER 4

IN THE FUTURE

Bioluminescence is found in different places in nature. Scientists are trying to use bioluminescence to make life easier for people. Bioluminescent trees could light city streets. Bioluminescent

LEARN MORE HERE!

Most bioluminescent creatures live in the ocean, but some live on land. Fireflies are bioluminescent creatures.

crops could glow to show they need water. Doctors are studying how to use the chemicals in fire plants to find diseases inside a person's body.

Plastic and other garbage is not good for the environment.

Millions of visitors to the Maldives **pollute** the sea surrounding the islands. This hurts the environment. If the **phytoplankton** die out, fish and other creatures will be threatened too.

If the environment is healthy, the Maldives can continue to be a good place for animals and plants to live.

Fire plants are found all over the world. But they are only able to glow in some places, like in the Sea of Stars.

Government leaders in the Maldives are working on ways to protect their islands and the ocean around them. They want to make sure that the lights in the Sea of Stars keep shining forever.

FUN FACT

Many creatures live in the ocean around the Maldives. The area has sharks, tropical fish, and coral.

OCEAN FOOD CHAIN

Phytoplankton are important. They are at the bottom of the ocean food chain. Krill and other small **organisms** need to eat phytoplankton to survive. Then, small fish eat the small organisms. Larger fish eat the small fish, and sharks eat the large fish. Without phytoplankton, this chain would be disrupted.

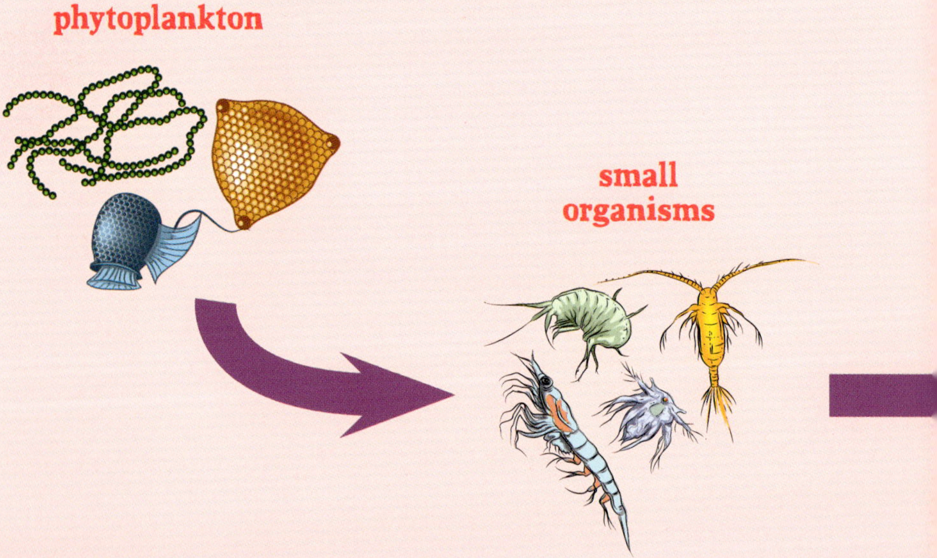

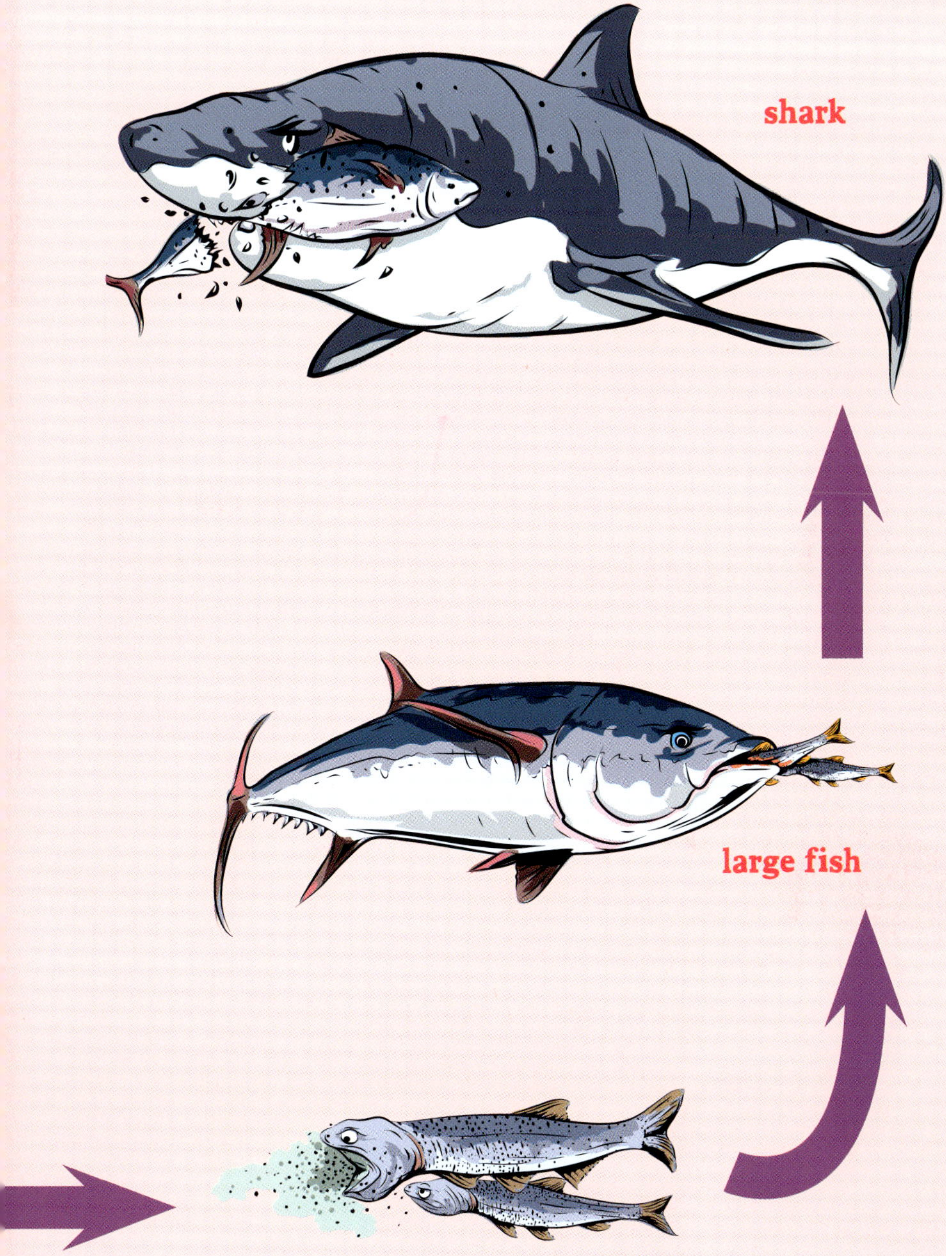
shark
large fish
small fish

MAKING CONNECTIONS

TEXT-TO-SELF

Would you want to visit the Sea of Stars? Why or why not?

TEXT-TO-TEXT

Have you read any other books about bioluminescent creatures? How and why do those creatures create light?

TEXT-TO-WORLD

Pollution is threatening phytoplankton. What are some things you can do to help reduce pollution?

GLOSSARY

bioluminescence — the ability of a living thing to make its own light.

dinoflagellate — a floating one-celled organism that lives in the ocean.

organism — one of various kinds of living things, including plants, animals, and very small life-forms.

photosynthesis — a process where plants produce their own food using sunlight.

phytoplankton — a tiny marine organism that is an important part of a food chain.

pollute — to put harmful chemicals or garbage where they don't belong, like in air or water.

predator — an animal that hunts other animals for food.

INDEX

ONLINE RESOURCES

popbooksonline.com

Scan this code* and others like it while you read, or visit the website below to make this book pop!

popbooksonline.com/sea-of-stars

*Scanning QR codes requires a web-enabled smart device with a QR code reader app and a camera.